For all who journey in faith, love and hope. May you find inner joy and fulfilment.

A huge thank you to all my family and friends who believe in me and have challenged me to share my poems with the world.

I love you all.

Reflections of the Soul
Introduction

At 16, I arrived in the United Kingdom with a combination of excitement, fears and aspiration for a better future.

Poetry came to me during the dark, challenging and exciting times of discovering who I was. An expression of my inner battles and frustrations with the world – deep thoughts I couldn't share or articulate with anyone.

Some of these poems came to me by divine spiritual inspiration and found their way to my soul, challenging me to give them a voice. For years, these poems were my secret therapy, my 'me' time, my friends that only came out to play when no one was watching. They have since journeyed with me these 49 years, giving me hope, joy, purpose and strengthened my faith when times were hard and I felt like giving up.

My fear of judgement kept the poems locked away for so long. Now I am ready to share them with you. As you meditate, ponder and immerse yourself in these poems, may you find INSPIRATION, EMPOWERMENT, SPIRITUALITY and a MINDSET of positive energy as you make of them what you must.

These poems are the 'Reflections of my Soul'.

ISBN 978-1-9996129-4-8
Copyright ©2018 Joy Ogeh Hutfield

The right of Joy Ogeh Hutfield to be identified as the author of this work has been asserted by her in accordance with the Copyright, Designs and Patents Act, 1988

All rights reserved. No part of this publication may be reproduced, stored in retrieval system or transmitted in any form or by any means electronic, mechanical, photocopying, recording or otherwise, without the prior permission of the publisher, except in the case of brief quotations embodied in critical articles and reviews.
A CIP record for this book is available from the British Library

This work is a work of fiction.
Names and characters are the product of the author's imagination and any resemblance to actual persons, living or dead, is entirely coincidental.

Published by
Llyfrau Cambria Books, Wales, United Kingdom.
Cambria Books is a division of
Cambria Publishing.
Discover our other books at: www.cambriabooks.co.uk

Cover design and portrait of the author by artist Prith Biant
Layout by Graham Davies, GD Graphics

Contents

INSPIRATION — 7

Lights of the night	8
Let me dream	9
Another day out to change the world	10
Crossroads	11
Reflection of the soul	12
Creation	13
Appreciation	14
A brand-new day	15
You	16
The perfect backdrop	17

EMPOWERMENT — 19

Life	20
When you look at me	21
I see	22
Step out	23
Journey to slavery	24
The sun will shine again	26
Mother	27
Nigeria	28
Africa	29
A letter from God	30
The result	31

MIND — 33

Let go	34
The devil within	35
Power	36
Legacy	37
The reaper	38
The mask	39

SPIRIT — 41

Welcome home	42
The voice	43
The legacy that lives on	44
Green trees	45
My faithful servant	46
Duty calls	47

INSPIRATION

"Keep your face always towards the sunshine and shadows will fall behind you"

Walt Whitman

Lights of the night

Lights of the dark
Like piercing eyes
Searching, watching, provoking
Lights in the dark
Assembled like soldiers ready for the worst
In unity, they march towards the battle field
Fighting, protecting, supporting
Lights of the night
Trees acting as soul mates
Houses as shields
Lights in the dark
Like eyes of the world
They know the meaning of life
Lights of the dark
Heads held high
Like proud peacocks
Not dared to be challenged
They signal, we obey
Their colours reflect the paths we should take
Red: danger
Yellow: life must never be debated
Green: life is worth more to those who trust
Lights of the night
Lights to the soul
Ease away the darkness
Set me free

Let me dream

Let me dream the dream that is me
A dream far removed from the past
A dream that searches the inner me
Needing to be awakened
Let me dream of peace, joy and laughter
A dream that enthuses, excites and motivates
Let me dream the dream that is me
A light slowly piercing through the darkness
Let me dream the dream that allows me to shine
A radiant light that even the darkness cannot contain
Let me dream the dream that is me
Making a difference, leading the way
Lighting the path of those who need to dream and dare to dream
Let me dream the dream that is me
The dream is now

Another day out to change the world

Another day out to change the world
Encountering different views, value streams and changing beliefs
Challenging self and others
Striving towards the love campaign
Holding on to the banner of hope and equality

Another day out to change the world
Fight back the tears not understanding the reasoning that lies
In the unspoken thoughts of discrimination and injustice
Facilitating the process of self-denial and self-evaluation
Exposing the power of destruction in the words we choose

Another day out to change the world
Pushing through, challenging the norms, refusing to stop
A vision of the love campaign
Standing side by side, tearing down the walls that say we can't
Running to the finishing line
Heaven's light shining through, embracing, welcoming
Another day out to change the world – I made it

Crossroads

I stand as an empty vessel before you
I have tried to fight my battles alone
I have reached that crossroad again
The path is so familiar
I am losing the battle again
I see your light wanting to shine through
Why do I still resist?
I come before your heavenly throne
I stand as an empty vessel before you
I have fought my battles and lost
I have reached that crossroad again
Fill my empty cup
Speak life into my soul
All I need is to be led by you
I have paid the price to reach the top
Aquiring everything yet unfulfilled
 I have lost the battle
I want to do things your way
I want to drink from your living water
That I might thirst no more

Reflection of the soul

Forgive me
Forgive me father
For the times I have doubted you
For the times I have failed to believe
For the times I could not see the plan for my life
For the times I could not see the bigger picture
For the times I hesitated, even when you called me to be yours

Thank you
Thank you father
For the times you ordered my footsteps
For the times I felt your hands pull me through life's messy pit
For the newness of life within my spirit and allowing me to abide under the shadow of your wings

Creation

The day was dawning
The birds flew majestically in awesome unity
They worshipped the Lord of Lords, the King of Kings
In great adoration of the mighty creator
They soared in confidence and freedom
In spiritual connection with the maker
They acknowledged His greatness with thanksgiving
They echoed with chants and praise
To the one who is worthy to be praised
Blessed be the name of the Lord

Appreciation

As you walk through those woods
Do not forget to say hello
To the trees that have graciously invited you in
As you sit on the beach
Remember to say thank you
To the sand that supported your body
As you lie down
With the sun shining on your face
Be kind and give a smile in appreciation and gratitude

A brand-new day

Every day is a brand new day
Grateful that I 'm awake, I'm alive
Grateful for being part of your day, part of your creation
I begin this day with love
An opportunity which might never come again
I choose to forgive
Freeing my mind to focus
Allowing my spirit to connect to the beauty and abundance that surrounds me

Every day is a brand new day
My soul commits to the goodness of God
The world has welcomed me into its fold
I am part of the solution as I journey on today
Empowering, inspiring , motivating all who travel with me
To create a better vision

Every day is a brand new day
The fear of yesterday no longer has a hold
My slate is wiped clean, to begin
I choose how my day begins
The day will not be wasted
A gift that will never be taken for granted
I live to tell the story of yet another day

You

There are men, and then there is you
A man made with Heavenly precision
Just for me
A heart designed to love me
Arms to hold me close
A smile to take away all my cares and worries
A man sent so that my joy may be complete
A soul mate that embodies the nature of Christ
Lifting, inspiring and empowering
Choosing to see the best
Persevering, standing by my side
Cheering me to the finishing line
A husband in whose eyes I see
My true reflection
I truly bless the day I found you
And in the Holy unity
We took our vows
You simply are God's gift to me.

Dedicated to my husband Mark.

The perfect backdrop

I woke up this morning
Feeling overwhelmed
Somewhat fed up with life itself
I opened the windows
A beautiful morning
As clouds moved gracefully across the waters
The trees stood majestically in awesome beauty
The birds flew with no care in the world

In the midst of my troubled self
I saw beauty
Real beauty

A calm voice spoke to me
'This is the perfect back drop for a perfect day'
I fell down on my knees
Overwhelmed, not by my feelings
But by his awesome presence

My life is the perfect back drop for a perfect day

EMPOWERMENT

"Nobody can go back and start a new beginning, but anyone can start today and make a new ending"

Maria Robinson

Life

Life is what you make it

Learn to see the love around you

With a servant's heart, serve all with humility and equality

Learn to walk in faith

Knowing your existence presents a solution to others

Live to be grateful for being part of creation

Let your smile be the key to someone's happiness

Keep your eyes focused on the beauty that radiates in all of us

Make life the centre of your universe

Uplifting, challenging, changing

Bringing joy, peace and abundance

Wake up, get excited

Clap your hands

Life is what you make it

Dare to trust

Dare to believe

Dare to be the best

Living the life that will never be lived twice

Life is what you make it

When you look at me

When you look at me
Do you see what you want to see?
Do you say what you want to say
When you look at me?

Do you see the hurt inside?
Do you feel the pain?
Do you see the tears running down my face
When you look at me?

Do you turn and walk away?
Do you say, 'Maybe someday I will lend you a hand'
Do you say, 'I cannot make a difference'?
Do you say, 'It's not my cause'?
When you look at me?

Can you stop to understand?
Can you let your actions say what you want to say?
Can you listen to my cries and help wipe away the tears
When you look at me?

Can you stand beside me, and say, 'It's time to make a difference'?

I see

I see what I see
I see the grass is green
I see the birds fly
I see the sun and the light it brings
I see the light and darkness that penetrate the graves
Their names tell a story
I see the path that I should take
I see the world as one
Don't ask me why I see
I see what I see

I see the making of life
From a new born into man
I see anger, greed and destruction
With our own hands, we destroy what we love the most

I see war, hatred and fears
I see tears, frustration and helplessness
Don't ask me why I see
I see what I see

I see the creation of a new world
I see peace, I see heaven
I see smiles, happy faces
I see a helping hand
It reaches out to everyone
I see hope, survival
I see the gentleness of hearts
Don't ask me why I see
I see what I see

Step out

You are living in the shadow of what you truly are
Afraid to take the next step of life
Afraid to trust the inner you
Living in the past that was yesterday's dream
You have created what you are now
Disappointed
      Frustrated
           Angry
Attributing blame to the things that never should have been
Take that step now
Make that decision count
Turn on the dream machine
Reinvent yourself
Wake up from your slumber
Stop chasing shadows
Who says you can't have it all?
Release yourself
Forgive your mistakes
Change is knocking at your door
Open the door
Be free
The future is great
Just live in it

Journey to slavery

The journey began with a shock
A deep awakening
A stillness of the soul
A hurt too painful for my fragile body to bear

A tear rolled from my numb face
A thousand tears wanted to follow
The numbness made it still

I could feel screams welling up inside me
My lips remained still
My thoughts made no sense
My reasoning, a bridge of confusion

I stared at my prison
The chains around my neck, hands, and feet
I was told I was now the property of a Mr Harrison
A branding on my back made with heated coals confirmed the fact

My life is no longer my own. I am no longer ME

With eyes that begged for mercy, I looked at my master
With every lash
My eyes grew bigger
My pain stronger
My spirit weaker

I fell to the ground
Knowing my pleading only made it worse
I couldn't stop myself
I burst into a chant
I chanted in my native language
It gave me comfort
My new master could never own my language

My voice got louder, louder, louder
A crashing blow to my head
I looked up, and saw a deep penetrating hatred in his face

I realised he would never see me as a human being
I was his property

The journey, which began as a shock, has ended in a time that will forever cause my heart to bleed

The sun will shine again

Wake up from your deep slumber
The sun will shine again
When all around you do not understand
When everything is falling apart
When your boat is in the middle of the storm
Your days are dark
Your nights deep blue
Fear takes the better of you
Anxiety becomes your best friend
Wipe away those tears
Your story is about to begin a new chapter
A special light is coming your way
Wading its way through the dark clouds
Peace is beckoning
Joy is descending
Look up
The sun is shining again

Mother

Precious is the woman
From whose womb I emerged
A mother gifted with grace
Marked and set aside
To impact and influence the world
A seed sown that would yield
A bountiful harvest in the hearts of men
A product of a prophecy that came to pass
A mother whose heart yields
To the instruction of the Almighty
A mother of all mothers
Called to service
To uphold the little ones
Always with open arms
Embracing and living the principles of equality for all
Mother, you are running the race
A true champion at heart
Never taking 'no' for an answer
A strong determined spirit
Who must reach the finishing line
I love you, mother
For you have taught me the true meaning of love

Dedicated to my mother Maria Ogeh.

Nigeria

Your children cry out
Where are you?
Where is the hand of peace?
That always held us together
That kept us warm from the harsh harmattan
Where is the wisdom that once spoke to our hearts?
Now our hearts are cold
Filled with hatred for one another
Where is our mother land
That made us a great nation
Now we mourn daily
Bodies now road blocks
Nigeria
Your children cry out
Wake up
Stand up
Wipe away our tears
Open a new chapter in our hearts
Mark it with love
Mark it with kindness
Mark it with peace
Mark it with solidarity
Bring us back together
North South East West
We must say a peaceful goodbye
To the hearts that do not belong

Africa

Yes! Africa, the place of my birth
The place which god has blessed
With all the fruitfulness of the earth
A place proud of its inhabitants

Africa, africa, the home of the beloved,
A place from where brave and mighty warriors spring
A place where customs and traditions are cherished

Africa, the home of my forefathers
The home of all god's creation

Yes! Africa, my africa
May your name be called with pride
For your sons and daughters have now come home.

A letter from God

Dear Joy,

I watched you as you closed your eyes to sleep
I took away all your cares and worries
I replaced them with peace
I opened your eyes this morning
So you can see the beauty
The provision I laid out for you
As you stepped out of bed
I whispered softly to you
'I love you'
As you got ready to start the day
I let you lean on my strength, wisdom and confidence
Your day was a success
Because I never took my eyes off you

Love
God

The result

I am a walking miracle
There is a hole in my heart
Pain so strong
I struggle to exist
Just when the monster thought it had a hold on me
I am a walking miracle
People came to see
People came to pray
People came to confirm
People came to speculate
People came to tell bad stories
People came to make me laugh
People came to laugh at me
People did not come at all

I am a walking miracle
Days of reflection
Days of prayer
Days of contemplation
Days of fear
Days of faith

I am a walking miracle
I am holding on
I am hanging on
I am clinging on
I am a walking miracle
I want to live
I want to love
I want to dance
I want to be free
I am a walking miracle
I am a life giving being
I am loving life
I am free
I am a walking miracle

MIND

"The face is the mirror of the mind and eyes without speaking confess the secrets of the heart"

St. Jerome

Let go

Let the rivers of forgiveness
Wash away the hurt the pain
You are so angry, so bitter
Seeking revenge
To punish, to pay back
You are plotting
Sowing lies
Wanting to get even
Yet deep down
You also are feeling the pain
Reaping the seed you have sown
You once loved and trusted
Now you are sick with jealousy
Twisted with envy
Wondering why happiness spits at you
Rewind the clock
It's time to start again
Put on a new outfit
Wear the garment of forgiveness
Let your feet be fitted with the shoes of peace
Wear the banner of love
The badge of kindness
Look into the mirror
Now, how about that for change?

The devil within

It starts with a smile
Barely touching the surface of the stomach
A taste is developed
A deep unexplained feeling to get even
It's exciting, and dangerously sweet
Guilt and consequences safely locked away
Judgement bribed for a later date
Jealousy, envy, hatred are entertained at the dinner table
Ruckus malicious laughter graces the atmosphere
Pain has excused itself and pleasure takes its position at the high table
Fake love sings in the background as the dagger is brought in
The unsuspecting victim dances to the tune
Intoxicated by the sweet romance
There's a sharp cry as the dagger pierces the heart
Jealousy, envy, hatred all stand to attention
The deed is done
Guilt unlocks itself
Pain is back
Judgement will not be bribed again
Judgement is here to stay
The price must be paid

Power

Your light is twinkling
About to go out
What have you done?
Darkness has crept into your soul
Your heart is filled with jealousy and pride
Wanting what others have
Their joy, peace, happiness and fulfilment
You prey on the vulnerable and unassuming
You love to put out their light
And watch them live in misery and confusion
You were once filled with light
You radiated love and joy
Now you battle between light and darkness
Darkness and light cannot co habit
Your light is fading
It's only a matter of time
What have you done?
Stop the evil schemes
Real power can never be found in these
Refuse the crown
There is still light inside of you
Allow it to shine out the darkness
Submit to the greater light
Let your soul live

Legacy

In your position of authority
You stepped upon my freedom
And repressed my rights
When I asked for help
In your position of comfort
You failed to see the injustice I suffered
In your narrow one dimensional vision
You found it difficult to accommodate my view point
In your position to influence change
You chose to do nothing
Knowing it caused me pain
In your legacy
You left none
You buried your head under the sand
You never stood up for anything
Your existence meant nothing
You left no legacy

The reaper

He that decides to bring others down
Will himself be brought down
Like a ton of bricks
For he has sown nothing good
In the hearts of men
When he had the chance
His reaping therefore will be in full
Until every life he has ruined
Is repaid in full
Be wise to sit on the side of justice

The mask

In pleasing others
You have created Jekyll and Hyde
You now stand in attention of your enemies
Wearing masks
That have never really defined you
You are smiling today
Crying tomorrow
You seek to please
In the places that destroy you
Now you are a skeleton of your former self
Not knowing who you are
You are a facade
Afraid of being found out
Your self-confidence has been trampled on
You are truly living the doormat experience
Afraid to ask the questions that matter most
Afraid to face the demons you have created
Have a personal relationship with yourself
Come back to you
The game is over
Appreciate the inner being that wants to love
Take off the masks
There is only one face
There is only one you
There is only one solution
Be at peace with yourself
And the world will be at peace with you

SPIRIT

"Sometimes you will never know the value of a moment, until it becomes a memory"

DR Seuss

Welcome home

In death we come to your Holy Throne
Our souls in total surrender
Our bodies no more in existence
Clothed in the robe that was soaked in the blood of the lamb
In righteousness we rise to meet the Saviour
In whose arms we truly belong
Death has not stolen us away
But reunited us with the Maker and the Author
For from dust we were made and to dust we must return
In chorus with the angels hallelujah
A new life has begun

The voice

I have been searching all my life
I have wanted so much from this world
As I rest in the depth of my thoughts
I heard a voice call out to me
I heard a voice call out my name
He said to me
'I have called you to be mine
I will lead you out of your darkness into light
I will be your eyes and pierce the souls of men
Seek me
Seek me with all your heart
Seek me
Seek me with all your soul
And I will never let you down
I will never keep anything away from you'

The legacy that lives on

He lived a life of service to others
Never complaining or questioning
He opened up his heart and mind daily to receive the abundance that life brought to him
So he could be a channel of blessings to all who encountered him
Creating the environment that made others feel special and secure
A man who lived with the fear of God
Walking diligently in the presence of the most high
His smile warmed the hearts of the cold hearted
His commitment empowered the lost and discouraged
His support restored the weak in spirit
A legacy of a man called to humbleness
That all may see the Christ that lived within him
A man of greatness, who touched the lives of others
And through his presence, gently ministered to their spirits
As the walls of Jericho fall flat to the ground
Arise, Dad, and stand upright
As the angels welcome you home and crown you with honour and life everlasting

Dedicated to my Father in law, Leslie Hutfield

Green trees

Green trees make a bed for me
My body is tired and weary
Fan me with your leaves and branches
Fan me to sleep
Let your gentle leaves sway me to sleep
Whilst listening to the beautiful music you make
Let the birds on your tree sing me a song
My weary body moving in rhythm
Let them echo in my ears
The meaning of life
I will sleep a beautiful sleep

My faithful servant

A life so precious
A greatness so much felt
By all who came in contact
Connected by Grace
She was the righteousness of the Father
A humble spirit, never assuming
But left a presence that touched and impacted many
A smile that whispered a thousand heartfelt words
That calmed every situation
A soul that loved the Lord
Quietly worshipping and exalting his mighty name
A life well spent
A legacy of love, respect and inner self assurance
A life called to service
In humbleness, giving to all
Margaret, be lifted up into the presence of the Almighty
As he whispers "Well done, my good and faithful servant".

A poem dedicated to Margaret

Duty calls

As Life slips away
The body is still
Overwhelm fills the mind
Of those who cannot and dare not
Understand the circle of life
Duty calls
Letting go cannot be comprehended
But as life slips away
It begs to be released
From Its pain
For there is no longer life
But an empty shell
Yet duty calls
Wanting to interrupt the process
To be selfish, wanted, acknowledged
Refusing Its all over
As breath slowly leaves the body
The soul is quiet
Perhaps no longer answerable
To the people of this world
No need to apologise
No guilt
No sadness
For it knows that
Duty no longer calls

About the Poet – Joy Ogeh-Hutfield

Joy was born in Nigeria in 1969 and came to the United Kingdom at the age of 16 years. She is the founder of Joy Transformation Coaching and now lives in Swansea, South Wales with her husband and three teenage children.

She started writing poetry at an early age and having some of her poems published in an anthology at the age of 17 years gave way to her performing her poems on various platforms across the U.K. In 2001, Joy was filmed by BBC Wales performing some of her poems written in Piggin English – Yanga de sleep, trouble come wake am.

Author of 'The Secrets to Motivating Your Team' and the life changing coaching workbook series 'Purpose Made Easy' and Joy Made Easy', Joy is also a multi-award winning transformation coach, international motivational speaker, T.V and radio personality with an infectious energy that leaves her audience inspired, empowered and motivated.

www.ingramcontent.com/pod-product-compliance
Lightning Source LLC
Chambersburg PA
CBHW071917160426
42813CB00098B/462